YOU CAN'T TAKE IT WITH YOU

How to protect your assets for many generations, not just one lifetime

By Matthew Mitchell

WRITE BUSINESS RESULTS

This book was produced in collaboration with Write Business Results Ltd.

www.writebusinessresults.com info@writebusinessresults.com

ISBN-13: 978-1979009898

ISBN-10: 1979009899

First published in the United Kingdom in 2017 via CreateSpace

Published by Legacy Legal Limited, Parallel House 32 London Road Guildford, Surrey GU1 2AB

For further information please visit www.legacylegal.co.uk or contact enquiry@legacylegal.co.uk

Contents

Foreword

This book contains really important information on how you can achieve one of the most important goals for any client in their lifetime. That goal being protecting the wealth you have amassed during your lifetime and ensuring it remains for your children, grandchildren and great grandchildren.

After reading this book you will no doubt ask the question 'Why hasn't anybody, including many of my professional advisers, told me this previously?'

This book explains very simply how everyday life events could have a devastating effect on you and your family.

Many people keep their fingers crossed and hope that these events do not happen to them or anyone in their family and don't consider that once the events covered in the book start there is little or nothing that can be done to stop your wealth being attacked and taken.

By reading this book you have taken the first step towards getting your estate planning affairs in order and protecting your wealth for many generations to come.

Clive Ponder BSc FIMMM. TEP

Introduction

Deciding whether to make your Will, and how to go about doing it, is one of the most important decisions you'll ever need to make. The process of making a Will, the purpose behind it, and what it can provide for you and your family can seem complicated.

With all the challenges life brings, it's not surprising that thinking about a Will isn't at the top of everyone's to-do list. But writing a Will needn't be a difficult, morbid process. In fact, it can give you peace of mind for the future, knowing that your assets that you have worked hard to accumulate throughout your life, even if most of that is in your home, is protected as fully as possible for your loved ones and future generations.

The book explains the importance of having a Will, and takes you through the process of making one. It talks about what life could be like for those left behind if you don't have one, putting you in a better position to make an informed decision about when and how to write your

Will. You'll find out the answer to pressing questions: important questions that you've probably asked yourself, but that have been pushed to the back of your mind. Questions such as:

- What will happen to my loved ones after I'm gone?
- Who will get my home and other assets?
- What will the government take?
- How can I find out about how to create a Will, and who can help me?

We'll address these questions and clear up some common misconceptions about estate planning: organising Wills, Trusts and Powers of Attorney.

I began my career as a financial adviser working for Legal & General, a top UK financial services company. Over a career of 20 years, I saw so many families whose lives were turned upside down when a member of the family died and they didn't have a Will in place. Looking back now I think about what a difference it would have made if my clients had just taken a little time to put a Will in place, and what a difference it would have made to their families future.

As a financial adviser my job was to organise life insurance, we were never trained to discuss estate planning with our clients. As is often the way in life, something happens that triggers a set of events, and for me it was when I lost a close friend to cancer at the age of 40. A few months before his passing he and his wife had asked me questions about writing a Will as they had just assumed it was part of the service I offered. After all why wouldn't it be, I'd spent years helping them grow their wealth, so why wouldn't I be able to help them protect it. I felt embarrassed when I had to admit it was a subject that I wasn't qualified to help them with and referred them to a friendly local estate planner. I felt that I had let them down but it was a seminal moment for me.

I realised from that day on that estate planning needed to be the foundation of all the work I was helping my clients with, rather than being an afterthought at the end of an appointment. To demonstrate this I would always draw a picture of a house, as below. I think it gets the concept of estate planning over in a clear and simple way:

Now this all sounds great, however, the problem was I had had no formal training in estate planning. I obviously knew what a Will was, but I had no idea of how to write one on behalf of a client.

As luck would have it I was introduced to a gentleman called Clive Ponder who owns and runs a very successful Wills & Trust corporation in the Midlands. Clive and I hit it off immediately and together we initiated a process that meant that I could do what I was good at – looking after my clients, and he could do what he was good at – estate planning. All we had to do was create a process where we could work together to ensure that clients got the best of both worlds and so that's what we did, and we are still working together to this day and seeing the numbers of people we are able to help grow monthly, which is wonderful to see. Clive has also kindly written the foreword to this book, for which I am very grateful.

In January 2016, the Law Society published a report about the future of legal services in the UK.[1] They highlighted the fact that the way people will buy legal services in the future will change. People are moving away from the traditional routes of getting their Will written, namely going to a solicitor, in favour of other channels that can offer the same service – for example via their financial adviser.

And so, with my association with a legal services company already in place and with lots of connections in the financial services industry, I brought the two together and formed a company called Legacy Legal Ltd. Together we help train financial advisers to offer an estate planning service to their clients. After all, as I knew from my own experience, it's a natural extension of what they do.

---

1 TheLawSociety,The Future of Legal Services (TheLawSociety:January2016)

We regularly hear that, when people write a Will, it's like a weight has been lifted from their shoulders. It's just the absolute relief, that they've sorted something they've been meaning to do for ages.

I like to think of estate planning as the missing piece of a financial jigsaw puzzle:

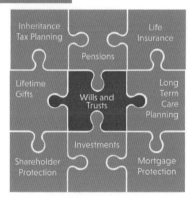

In this book, I want to give you a balanced view of estate planning to empower you to make the right decision about when and how to write your Will.

'Dream as if you'll live forever, live as if you'll die tomorrow',

James Dean

Part One

Wills Made Simple

Do you have a Will? If not, you're not alone. Two thirds of people in the UK don't have one.

If you do have a Will, when did you last review and update it?

Often, I talk to people who might've made their Will 30 years ago. In that time they could've moved house two or three times, had children who have grown up, got married and had children of their own. A lot happens over the course of a lifetime, and a Will you made 30 years might not reflect your wishes today. With everything life brings us — birth, death, marriage, divorce — it's no surprise that writing or updating your Will doesn't seem like a priority.

Writing a Will can seem daunting. Many people associate it with death, and understandably, don't like to consider it. However, writing a Will is actually a simple process. It can give you peace of mind and protect your legacy for your loved ones.

Whoever you are and whatever your circumstances, you no doubt have people that you care about and that are important in your life. That is true of all of us. These may be members of your family, your spouse or partner, your children, grandchildren, parents, etc. You may also have close friends that you trust and care about.

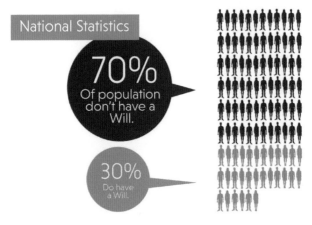

National Statistics

70%
Of population don't have a Will.

30%
Do have a Will.

So, what exactly is a Will, and how do you go about making one?

A Will is a document that clearly outlines who you would want to benefit from your estate in the event of your death. It doesn't have to be in a formal document, it can be written on any piece of paper. You simply state what you'd like to happen to your estate and nominate an executor. To be valid, a Will needs to be signed and witnessed by two independent people. If you have children who will be under the age of 18, you can name someone as their legal guardian to take care of them and make arrangements to provide for them financially. Having a Will in place also ensures that your estate passes through Probate quickly.

However, remember that for a Will to be valid. It must be:

- Signed by Testator (the person writing the Will)
- Dated.
- Witnessed by 2 adults who are NOT Beneficiaries or the spouse of a beneficiary in the presence of the Testator and each other.

Your Will allocates several roles to people, and you will need to give some serious thought as to who will be able to fulfil them. They are:

- Executors
- Guardians
- Beneficiaries
- Trustees

What makes up an estate?

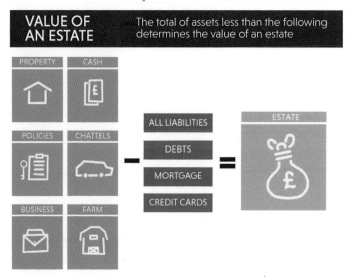

VALUE OF AN ESTATE	The total of assets less than the following determines the value of an estate

PROPERTY · CASH · POLICIES · CHATTELS · BUSINESS · FARM — ALL LIABILITIES · DEBTS · MORTGAGE · CREDIT CARDS = ESTATE

Your estate is all of your assets: your house or flat (in the UK or overseas), shares, savings, investments as well as your personal possessions. The value of your estate is worked out by calculating the total value of your assets, minus any liabilities, including your mortgage, debts and credit cards.

Upon your death it is the role of the executor to deal with your estate according to your wishes, to ensure that your loved ones get what you intended.

However, being an executor isn't really an honour, it can be a difficult and time consuming job that carries personal legal liability.

Your executor could be a surviving spouse or partner, a friend, family member or a professional such as a solicitor or accountant. Ideally, they should be familiar with financial matters, and be willing and able to take on the responsibility of the role.

The executors role is to settle off and close down all your affairs with the government, and get what's called a 'Grant of Probate'. Probate is the first stage in the administration of a Will. It's worth noting that all estates over £5,000 go through Probate whether there is a Will or not.

The executor must provide the Probate registry with:

- The most recent Will
- The family tree
- Current evaluation of the assets of the deceased which Probate pass to the HMRC

Once this has been done the executor must follow the order of administration of the Will as follows:

- Pay any debts
- Distribute any legacies
- Distribute the residue (What's left)

What is the purpose of a Will really?

———

Ok, so we've covered the basics of what a Will is and what it does. But what's the real purpose of writing a Will, and why should you do it now?

Well, much of your life is spent accumulating possessions: buying a house, saving for the future, planning for retirement and collecting 'priceless treasures' that have more sentimental than intrinsic value. It is only natural that you would want to pass those things on to the people that you care about most. So, if you want to keep your assets safe, it is important to make sure that you have put as much protection in place as possible while you are still able to do so.

If a partner in a relationship were to die, all sorts of painful emotions surface bringing various considerations into play. The partner left behind may think, do I need, or want, to move house? Do I move area? What will my life be like now? What do I do on a day-to-day basis? How will I get by? Death is final: that person is gone and is not around to help or talk to anymore. That's when you need people you know, love and trust around you to help you make decisions that are going to be the right choices for you at a time when you're clearly going to be vulnerable.

Fundamentally, that's why making sure that the paper-work, for want of a better expression, is right and all in-order, so that there are clear instructions to the executor about what to do. By writing a Will and making sure you review it when your circumstances change, you are safeguarding your loved ones from unnecessary future emotional stress and financial worries.

Why is having a Will important?

Let's look at the purpose and importance of having a Will in a bit more detail.

It's a common misconception that assets automatically pass to a spouse or registered civil partner on death. However, if you don't have a Will in place your estate will be distributed under the UK rules of intestacy, which means that the law decides who inherits your estate and in what proportions. In effect, the government has written a Will for you – imagine that. It will almost certainly contradict what your wishes would have been.

It might as well read as follows:

To my Family

I hereby leave you all several months, possibly years, of financial hardship and expense, whilst you go to unnecessary lengths to sort out my affairs.

To my Spouse/Partner

I hereby leave you some, (but probably not all) of what I own.

To my Children

I hereby leave you the remainder of my Estate and give you the authority to enforce the sale of any part of it (including the family home) to realise your inheritance.

To Social Services

If my children are orphaned, I give you the authority of Guardianship and the power to choose who shall look after them, including allocating them to foster parents.

To the Tax Man

I hereby leave you all the Tax that I could have avoided and given to my family.

To the local authority

I hereby authorise the local authority to force the sale of my house and to liquidate any investments I have to pay for my care and save the local authority funds for projects more important than me. I realise that this could make the local authority one of the major Beneficiaries to my estate.

To my family who desperately need state funded benefits for any disability

I hereby authorise you to pay funds to any of my disabled beneficiaries so the state can then save money which they can then give to others not related to me. I realise that this could make the state one of the major Beneficiaries to my estate.

To my children and grandchildren

I hereby authorise you to ensure that if the children and/ or grandchildren get divorced that half of what I left them is payable to the ex in laws after the divorce proceedings, and they have ample money to look after the new spouse and any children they may have. I realise that this could make my divorced ex in laws one of the major Beneficiaries to my estate.

To my Bank and/or Solicitor

I hereby authorise you to charge whatever you feel necessary, to sort out the mess that I have left behind. I realise that this could make you one of the major Beneficiaries to my estate.

To everyone else

I leave you nothing!

So as you can see, dying intestate probably isn't something most people would choose. Ok, so the spouse, partner and biological children will get something after all the mess has been sorted out. However, it doesn't make provision for unmarried partners, step children, friends, pets and charities. Without a Will your property and possessions may end up in the hands of those who you may not have wished to inherit.

If you have dependent children, consider this question:

'In the event of your death, who would you like to look after your children?'

Before you answer that, take a look at this. Which of the groups below would you think the law constitutes as *your* children?

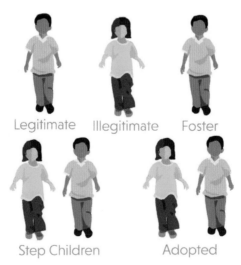

Legitimate   Illegitimate   Foster

Step Children   Adopted

The answer is

Legitimate
Illegitimate
Adopted

Step Children
Foster

Did you get it right?

When asked 'Who would you like to look after your children after you've gone?', more often than not the reply comes back as a family member or close friend. However, the reality is that without having a Will in place the children will be taken into state care. Family members or close friends will come forward but the council will not release the children until they have had time to do their background checks and make sure they are fit to be guardians.

People are understandably horrified and confused by this. They'll point out that their family member or friend knows their children, and already looks after them frequently. But the point is that the local council don't know that, they don't know your family member or friend, and there's no document anywhere proving the connection between them and your children.

Now, given that councils tend to be under a huge amount of pressure, this process can take months.

If you have children or know people with dependent children, how would you feel about them going into care for an undetermined period of time. Obviously, it's a situation that is unthinkable even for a day, let alone a month or three months.

The good news is that this can be completely avoided simply by writing a Will.

Writing a Will allows you to nominate your preferred guardians, people you trust with your children. Once you have nominated guardians, it's a good idea to make sure that they have some money for the purpose, as bringing up children is expensive. We would recommend that you speak with your financial adviser to make sure you have adequate life insurance in place to ensure that your children are adequately provided for.

So let's recap on what could happen if you don't have a Will:

- Your property and possessions may end up in the hands of those you may not want to have inherited.

- Your spouse or registered civil partner and children could end up with less than you had hoped.

- People you would like to inherit from your estate may not actually benefit.

- Your loved ones' inheritance may be subject to an Inheritance Tax bill, that could have been reduced or mitigated altogether with prior planning.

- Delays may occur in winding up your estate causing prolonged grief.

Having got this far in the book, I'm sure you will agree that having a Will is one of the most important things you can do for yourself and your family. Not only can a Will legally protect your spouse, children and assets, it can also spell out exactly how you would like things handled after you have passed away.

While each person's situation varies, here are just a few reasons to write a Will:

- You decide how your estate will be handled upon your death, putting you in control of who gets what

- You decide who will take care of your children by appointing guardians you know and trust

- You speed up the probate process and avoid unnecessary delays

- You decide who will wind up the affairs of your estate by nominating executors

- You can disinherit individuals who would otherwise stand to inherit by specifically outlining how you would like your estate to be distributed

- You prevent your loved ones from having to go through legal challenges after your death

- You can change your mind if your life circumstances change (It's a good idea to review your Will every two years or sooner if any of the following events occur):

1. Death of a beneficiary
2. Marriage of the testator or testatrix
3. Divorce of testator or testatrix
4. Move home
5. Marriage/Divorce of a beneficiary
6. Change in financial circumstances
7. Retirement of the testator or testatrix

Given how important a Will is – not only from a financial perspective but also bearing in mind family arrangements – what stops so many people from having one?

Why don't people have a Will?

Fear is a significant factor. People don't want to think about it, so they avoid doing it. Fear often leads to superstitions. People can be afraid that writing a Will may 'jinx' them — that in some way it means signing their own death warrant. If they think about it and act on it, it will somehow bring death closer. It's completely understandable to be fearful and superstitious, but our experience shows that confronting this fear and writing a Will gives people a great sense of relief.

Hopefully we will all lead long and healthy lives, but none of us knows when we're going to die. Planning to write your Will some time in the future is a bit like assuming that you're going to be given an advance warning before dying. This probably isn't going to be the case, and even if it was, wouldn't you rather spend your limited time with your loved ones, rather than trying to sort out your Will? The only thing that we know for sure is that death will happen at some point. It's better to sort out your Will now, today, so that you can live your life to the full with one less thing to think about.

Then you can simply review it every two years to make sure that it still reflects your wishes following all the changes life brings.

There are also a lot of misconceptions about Wills — how to make them and what they mean. For example, many people don't know that marriage invalidates a Will. Say both you and your partner made a Will individually when you were single. You buy a house, then you get married. Your Wills would then be invalidated.

Now, all of a sudden, Little Johnny's come along. As we mentioned earlier, you now have more things to consider when it comes to writing a Will. For example, in the event of your death, who will be Johnny's guardians? If you leave all of your money to Johnny, are you going to put restrictions on when he can have it? Say you were to die when Johnny was 18, and the value of your estate is a million pounds. Can he have it all then? Or would you want to put something in place to say that, between the ages of 18 and 25, there's a temporary trustee in place that basically looks after the money on his behalf?

Of course, when you're getting married, you're not thinking about Wills. You're too caught up in the happy moments, and when you're having your first child, you have a thousand and one other priorities and happy thoughts. Thinking about a Will seems morbid and unnecessary.

However, you know that you're going to get round to writing a Will one day. It's just a case of when. You're not not going to do it in your lifetime, so why don't you just get it out of the way and do it now? Do it right the first time, and review it every two years to keep it up to date.

We often hear clients saying they're too young to have to think about it. If you're a fit, healthy 25, 35 or 45 year old, why do you need a Will? You're not planning on dying anytime soon, so why bother? Thankfully, it's obviously less common for younger people to pass away, but nobody knows what might happen and when.

Remember, writing a Will is not something to leave for your deathbed. As I mentioned right at the start of the book, your Will should be the foundation of other financial arrangements, including mortgages, pensions and life insurance, since it outlines and protects what belongs to you: your assets that you work so hard to create. Your Will therefore isn't one, static document. It is something that changes over the course of your lifetime.

After fear, probably the most common reply when asked 'Why don't you have a Will ?' is not knowing who to ask. Many people think that they need to see a solicitor to make a Will. It's not uncommon for someone to have only ever used a solicitor when they buy a house or move home, and since this type of solicitor tends to specialise in conveyancing, they have little experience of estate planning.

Whilst we're on that subject, there is a difference between discussing writing your Will with a solicitor, who you may or may not know, and dealing with your financial adviser, who is also a qualified estate planner and whom you have known for many years.

For example, let's say you decided to go and see a solicitor. You don't know one and so you have to get a number from the Yellow Pages, book an appointment in their office at a time that suits them between 9 and 5 Monday to Friday, and you go and see them.

Here's how the conversation with the solicitor would go:

'I'd like to write a Will please'.

'What would you like your Will to say?'

'I'd like to leave everything to my wife and she would like to leave everything to me, then we'd like it to go to our children'.

The solicitor will take your instructions, draft the Will and charge you accordingly. On the face of it this seems perfectly reasonable as you got what you asked for (even if you're not really sure what that was).

Alternatively, you could book an appointment with your financial adviser who is qualified to discuss estate planning, in the comfort of your own home at a time to suit you.

As your financial adviser they already have a good understanding of your assets and an idea of the value of your estate, a fact that the solicitor may not take into account.

Upon completing a short questionnaire, client's details are sent to legal experts, who produce a bespoke estate planning report. The adviser would then present the report to the client at a convenient time and talk through the recommendations step-by-step in order to fully protect their client's estate and take instructions according to the client's wishes.

Given the two scenarios which would you choose?

Typically all estate planning reports will include a combination of Wills, Trusts and Powers of Attorney. In the next section we will show you some examples of why having a stand alone Will is a good start but may not provide the security you require. That's where trusts come into play.

What is a Trust?

─────

So, what exactly is a trust? We'll go into this in more detail later on in the book but in simple terms, a trust is a legal document that allows one person to hold assets (which can be almost anything) to which another person is entitled, while the trust itself technically 'owns' them.

Part Two

Life Stories

We've looked at what a Will is and why so many people don't have one. Fears, not knowing who to ask, and life events taking precedence all add up to stop people from writing a Will. However, getting on top of it can give you and your family reassurance, security and peace of mind. Plus, if you use an estate planner, you'll have the added confidence that you're making the best decision for you.

If you're still unsure about the importance of writing a Will, consider these questions:

- How would you feel if your assets ended up in the hands of someone you had never met?

- Would you be happy for your grandchildren to pay Inheritance Tax on assets they may receive in the future from you and on which you may have already paid inheritance tax on? This is called Generational Inheritance Tax

- What would happen to their inheritance if one of your children divorced after your death?

- Who would you trust to look after your affairs if you were no longer able to manage them?

In this section, we're going to address these questions and think about the importance of estate planning in more detail. We'll look at why having a Will that leaves everything 'absolutely' to your beneficiary may not be the right thing to do.

To demonstrate this we have 3 scenarios and are going to use a fictitious couple called Paul & Kate and their two children Charlotte and Jessica, both aged 8.

PAUL AND KATE: SCENARIO 1

Paul and Kate are married and have two children, Charlotte and Jessica. They've been meaning to write a Will for a long time but life has just got in the way. However, due to a recent death in the family they have decided that it's time to finally get their Will sorted.

Having visited a local solicitor they decide to leave everything to each other and then to their daughters, Charlotte and Jessica (Sound familiar?)

Paul has died, and as per his wishes he left everything in his Will to Kate. This includes his half of the house, his pension, his cash, his investments and his life insurance — everything. He wants to do this so that Kate can continue to look after and provide for Charlotte and Jessica.

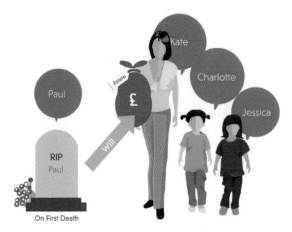

Life moves on and after some time, Kate meets somebody else. Let's call this somebody else, just for ease of explanation, Mr. New.

Kate marries Mr. New but forgets that marriage revokes a Will and so she now has no Will.

Unfortunately, things don't go too well for Kate and she decides to divorce Mr. New. As a result she loses 50% of everything she owns through the divorce proceedings.[2] So effectively, half of the money that Paul left Kate now belongs to Mr. New.

Worse still, let's just say that, before they get divorced, Kate dies. Without a Will in place Kate will have died In-testate meaning that Mr. New is now potentially going to get everything, leaving Charlotte and Jessica with very little or nothing at all.

2 Please note, the figures and percentages used in the 3 scenarios are for illustrative purposes only and cannot be taken or seen as being given advice.

To see a real life example of this take a look at the case of Lynda Bellingham, the much loved actress from the Oxo adverts. After Lynda's death in 2014, her husband and sons became embroiled in a bitter battle over her £5million estate, with her sons claiming that her husband had taken control of her assets and splurged their inheritance.[3]

Is that really something Paul and Kate would have chosen if they had known?

PAUL AND KATE: SCENARIO 2

Paul dies and he leaves everything to Kate. Kate then dies and leaves everything equally to Charlotte and Jessica.

On first death

On second death

---

3 See http://www.dailymail.co.uk/news/article-3536017/Lynda-bellingham-s-widower-hits-row-sons.html

Charlotte gets married, but sadly gets divorced. As we saw in an earlier example, Charlotte could lose 50% of everything she inherited from her mum and dad, Paul and Kate, in the divorce settlement.

Jessica receives her inheritance. She goes into business. There's a massive drop in the economy and unfortunately, through no fault of her own, she loses her business. The bankruptcy courts could potentially come after 100% of her inheritance.

So, in one generation, up to 100% of the assets that Paul and Kate worked so hard for has just been lost, through either divorce or bankruptcy.

Is that really something they would have chosen? If there was a way to protect against the eventualities do you think that Paul and Kate would have at least wanted to consider it?

Now ask yourself this: if that was to happen to your family, how would you feel?

PAUL AND KATE: SCENARIO 3

Paul has lost mental capacity. He hasn't appointed anybody to act as an Attorney on his behalf regarding his finances or health and welfare.

Kate and their now adult children Charlotte and Jessica wish to make those decisions on his behalf, however, legally they have no authority.

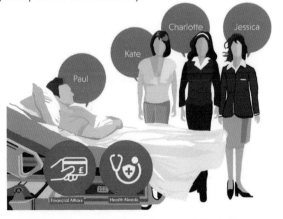

'Could I still get money from our joint bank account to pay the bills?'

It's a common misconception that if you have a joint bank account, and one of you loses mental capacity, your partner can just go and get the money out of the bank.

Here is what the British Bankers Association say in their leaflet on managing a bank account for someone else:

If one joint account holders loses mental capacity, banks and building societies can decide whether or not to temporarily restrict the use of the account to essential transactions only (e.g. living expenses and medical or residential care bills) until a Deputy has been appointed or a Power of Attorney registered.[4]

As you can see, without having a power of attorney in place the shutters come down not only for banks but also other organisations in control of your finances. They want to see the power of attorney document to ensure that the partner has the authority to access the bank account. Without this document, banks have to go through their due process, which takes weeks, if not months.

This is why having powers of attorney in place are a crucial part of estate planning.

---

4 British Bankers Association, Guidance for people wanting to manage a bank account for someone else. Available at: https://www.bba.org.uk/publication/leaflets/guidance-for-people-wanting-to-manage-a-bank -account-for-someone-else-2/

Again, as with writing your Will, this is not something to leave until the last minute. Sometimes, for example, we get enquiries such as this: 'We are taking mum to see the doctor tomorrow afternoon as she is beginning to get quite forgetful and we're worried about her. We've been meaning to contact you for some time to pop over and sort out her power of attorney. Is there any chance you could come and see us in the morning before we leave?'

There's a case law that dates back to 1870 in the name of 'Banks vs Goodfellow' which basically states that the person writing the Will or Power of Attorney must feel confident that the person making the Will or Power of Attorney has got mental capacity. The Mental Capacity Act 2005 complements this earlier rule, and states that an individual should be assumed to have mental capacity unless proved otherwise. Whenever capacity is in question the application to the Office of the Public Guardian must always be sent along with a letter from a qualified person stating that the client has capacity.

Registering a power of attorney can take a number of weeks, there's no urgent cases, no fast track or VIP service. They are processed in strict date order.

And so, going back to our example, Paul had not arranged power of attorney, meaning his family could not make key decisions on his behalf or manage his affairs for him. And so, everyday events like paying the mortgage or even for the weekly shopping may be affected.

These 3 scenarios happen every day. It's not very pleasant to put yourself in Paul and Kate's shoes. Maybe you've thought about some of these potential scenarios before, or know of someone who has experienced them.

The good news is all of these situations are avoidable. We may not be able to dodge death, but we can certainly side-step the unnecessary future emotional stress and financial worries that comes from not having strategies in place.

Effective estate planning doesn't mean 'giving it all away' or putting your own financial security at risk in favour of future beneficiaries. It does, however, give you the peace of mind of knowing that whatever happens in the future, you or those you trust will remain in control of your assets now and after you have died or lost mental capacity.

Structured in the right way, your estate planning will ensure that only the people you choose will be your beneficiaries. Nobody else will be able to make a claim against your estate or take the assets from them.
How much better will you feel knowing that you've planned for these contingencies? The next part of the book tells you exactly how to do that.

Part Three

Your Will, Made Easy

We've looked at why you might write a Will, and you've considered what could happen if you don't. We've also looked at what could happen when one loses mental capacity and the effects that could have on everyday living.

So, here are the 4 simple steps to getting your estate planning affairs in order.

Step 1: Write a Will

The first step of the process is simply to act on what you already know: that having a Will is important so book an appointment to see your financial adviser at your earliest convenience.

As you'll know from the previous section of this book, this first step is going to involve making difficult choices and facing up to difficult facts. You're going to have to talk about you dying, about who is going to be the executor, and who, if applicable, will act as guardians and look after your children.

Step 2: Set up Trusts

In Part 2 of the book we looked at 3 scenarios where Paul and Kate had written a Will leaving their estate to each other and then to the children.

In each of the scenario's we posed the question 'If this were to happen to you and your family, how would you feel?'

Setting up trusts would have prevented any of the assets passing outside of Paul and Kate's estate. So, let's look again at each of the 3 scenarios but this time, rather than Paul and Kate writing a Will leaving their assets 'absolutely' to each other, their Will directs their assets to a trust. This ensures that the assets will stay with Charlotte and Jessica and onwardly to their grandchildren. We refer to this as 'Bloodline Planning'.

What is a Trust?

As we've discussed, when you write a Will, you direct your assets to your beneficiary. They either go to your beneficiary in 'absolute' terms, or they go into a trust.

A trust is a legal concept that started in the Crusades in the 11th century. If you were recruited to go off and fight, you could be away for years, and the chances of you coming home were slim. So, you'd entrust a neighbour to look after your land and other assets; they would benefit from using them and you would benefit from knowing they are protected.

Over the centuries this type of arrangement has developed into a robust mechanism used worldwide. They can be found in everyday life, for example, if you have a pension. By using trusts to protect your assets, you are able to specify how and when your beneficiaries will receive a benefit from your estate. You can impose conditions or time limits on gifts to individual members of your family. This can be of enormous benefit to their long-term security.

Roles within a trust

- **Settlor** – The person who has established the trust
- **Beneficiary** – The person who will benefit from the trust
- **Trustee** – The person who looks after and manages the trust on behalf of the beneficiaries. Note that the trustee and beneficiary can be the same person, for example a spouse.

A trust serves to protect your assets for your loved ones. Rather than giving one person everything in absolute terms, you put your assets into a trust that is managed by your appointed trustees for the benefit of the beneficiaries. It's a bit like having a treasure chest, and giving someone the key. Effectively, a trust is a legal document that says, 'I give this person the rights to use the assets in my trust when I die'.

You might be thinking, 'why not just give the person your assets outright, instead of just giving them access to it?' Well, remember what happened when Paul gave Kate everything in scenario 1 earlier? Kate lost 50% of the assets inherited from Paul, and Charlotte and Jessica potentially lost up to 100%.

Using the picture below, let's work through the scenario again and take a look at what would have happened if Paul had directed his assets into a trust for the benefit of Kate.

Paul has died, his Will directs his assets to a trust where Kate is the trustee and also the beneficiary.

As the trustee Kate is allowed to take assets out of the trust (property, cars, money) and issues herself a 'Loan Note' – now this is important as these assets do not belong to Kate, in effect she's only borrowed them, they are not hers.

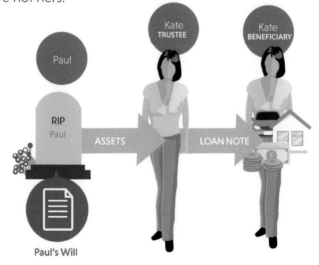

You'll remember Kate then married Mr New but later got divorced at which time she lost 50% of what she had inherited from Paul.

However, with a trust in place because Kate has only borrowed assets from Paul's trust (don't forget Kate has a loan note which says she's got to pay back what she's taken) Mr New isn't entitled to any of Kate's inheritance.

Now in Paul's trust he also stated that once Kate had passed away he would like Charlotte and Jessica to be the trustees and beneficiaries. These are called 'Reserves' and Kate did the same with her planning.

In scenario 2 Paul and Kate have both passed away leaving their assets equally between Charlotte and Jessica. However, this time they had written a Will that directed the assets into a trust.

Let's take a look at what would have happened to Charlotte and Jessica's inheritance now.

As we saw in scenario 1, Charlotte and Jessica are both the trustees and the beneficiaries.

Like their mum Kate they take assets out of the trusts using loan notes – meaning the assets are not theirs.

So in scenario 2 Charlotte gets married and then divorced, but because Paul and Kate have left their assets in trust for Charlotte they are not taken into account when calculating a divorce settlement, as the assets are not hers, they belong to the trust. And so Charlotte retains 100% of the assets.

Let's take a look at how this would have affected Jessica. You'll recall that Jessica lost 100% of her inheritance when her business failed and the bankruptcy courts took everything.

The same applies here as in Charlotte's case. Because the assets belong to a trust that Jessica is the beneficiary of, they do not count as part of her estate and therefore cannot be taken into account for any bankruptcy proceeding, saving 100% of her inheritance.

By writing a Will and directing your assets to a trust you will be able to protect against:

Marriage after death

Should the surviving spouse re-marry, those assets cannot be taken into the second marriage. This removes any threat of the children being disinherited.

The survivor is still able to use the assets in the trust in their lifetime.

Divorce

Placing the assets into a trust on death ensures that, if the children or chosen beneficiaries are subject to divorce proceedings, the inheritance they received is protected in any divorce settlements.

Creditors and Bankruptcy

Placing the assets into a trust on death ensures that, if any beneficiaries are subject to creditor claims or even bankruptcy, their inheritance cannot be taken into account in any claims.

Further Generational Inheritance Tax

Holding the assets in the discretionary trust ensures that they do not add to the beneficiaries' estate and therefore cannot be included in any Inheritance Tax assessments on the beneficiaries estate.

Step 3: Power of Attorney

As we touched on in scenario 3 when Paul lost mental capacity things began to get very tough for Kate and their daughters Charlotte and Jessica.

Lasting Powers of Attorney (LPA) are considered to be as important as Wills, allowing your affairs to be managed efficiently, in line with your wishes, if you are incapacitated by accident or illness at anytime during your lifetime.

It is important to set up an LPA while you are still mentally capable, well before you need it. If you become mentally incapacitated later in life and don't have LPAs in place, your relatives can face long, distressing delays and expense in applying to the court to take control.

There are two types of LPA:

- Property and Financial Affairs
- Health and Welfare

Property and Financial Affairs

A Property and Financial Affairs LPA allows you to choose one or more persons to make decisions about your money or property on your behalf. This includes fulfilling important tasks such as paying bills, writing cheques, transferring money, receiving salaries, arranging for the upkeep of your property or even selling it, if necessary.

Health & Welfare

A Health and Welfare LPA allows you to appoint one or more persons to make decisions regarding your medical care, moving into a care home, your daily routine (for example, eating and what to wear) and refusing life-sustaining treatment. Unlike the Property and Financial Affairs LPA it can only be used once you have lost the ability to make your own decisions.

Lets take a look at the roles within the Power of Attorney:

Donor – Person establishing the Power of Attorney.

Attorney – Person appointed by the Donor to help make decisions or to make decisions on their behalf.

Certificate Provider – The Certificate Provider must ensure that the person who wishes to make the LPA is mentally capable of making that LPA and that there is no pressure on them to make one.

Who can be your attorney

Your attorney needs to be 18 or over. They could be:

- A relative
- A friend
- A professional, for example a solicitor
- Your husband, wife or partner

You must appoint someone who has the mental capacity to make their own decisions.

Your attorney doesn't need to live in the UK or be a British citizen.

When choosing an attorney, think about:

- How well they look after their own affairs, for example their finances
- How well you know them
- If you trust them to make decisions in your best interests
- How happy they will be to make decisions for you

If there's more than one attorney

If you're appointing more than one person, you must decide if they'll make decisions:

- Separately or together - sometimes called 'jointly and severally' - which means attorneys can make decisions on their own or with other attorneys
- Together - sometimes called 'jointly' - which means all the attorneys have to agree on the decision

You can also choose to let them make some decisions 'jointly', and others 'jointly and severally'.

Attorneys who are appointed jointly must all agree or they can't make the decision.

Who can be a Certificate Provider?

There are two types of Certificate Provider. A knowledge based provider, which is someone who has known the Donor personally for over two years, or a skills based provider who has the relevant professional skills and expertise to enable them to make a judgement about mental capacity.

For a skills based provider the acceptable categories are:

- A registered healthcare professional
- A solicitor or barrister
- A registered social worker
- An Independent Mental Capacity Advocate (IMCA) or
- Someone not from the above list that can show what their relevant professional skills and expertise in determining mental capacity are

Skills based providers are entitled to charge a fee for providing the certificate.

Powers of Attorney must be registered before they can be used. This is done through the Office of the Public Guardian for a fee of £82 per document and can take up to 12 weeks.[5] Registration of your documents is optional, but strongly recommended, because of how long it takes to complete the registration process. If there is a problem with your documents during the registration process and you have already lost capacity, it may be too late to make corrections.

Summary

Writing a Will, setting up a trust and registering powers of attorney can be difficult things to think about that you're going to need to invest some of your time into. But, at the end of it, you're going to have a document that truly reflects your wishes. Financial advisers who have been trained to help their clients with estate planning have good knowledge of their clients' situation and are well placed to make sure that the correct planning is in place.

5 If the donor's gross annual income is less than £12,000, they may be eligible for a 50% reduction of the fee. These figure are accurate at the date of publication. See https://www.gov.uk/government/publications/power-of-attorney-fees

Step 4: Next Steps

Going back to the start of the book, the process of estate planning begins with booking an appointment to discuss writing a Will, or if you've done a Will that you haven't reviewed for some time, reviewing it to make sure that the decisions you made at the time are still relevant now.

Once your Will, Trusts and Powers of Attorney have been executed, it is important that you take steps to store the originals securely.

In particular if your Will is damaged or defaced, the Probate Registry may consider that an attempt has been made to revoke it and may refuse to admit it to probate. In either case, your estate may be treated as if you had not made a Will at all – and this will mean you will be deemed to have died intestate where the rules of intestacy will then come into play. You could consider storing your documents at a dedicated secure storage facility where they will be stored in waterproof, tamper-evident wallets, insured against loss and can be retrieved when you need them.

This book has taken you through the process of writing a Will. From thinking about your assets, to seeking advice, to holding the piece of paper in your hand, ready to be reviewed regularly to keep it up to date.

Your Will sets out who you want to benefit from your estate and in what way you want them to benefit. So, what's stopping you from having a Will? For your own peace of mind, talk to your financial adviser today about writing your Will, and setting up trusts and powers of attorney thereby protecting your future and laying the foundations of financial security for you and your family.

About the Author

After working as a financial adviser for over 20 years, Matthew Mitchell began a career as an Estate Planner.

Building on his experience of organising life insurance for his clients, and seeing the devastating effects that not having a Will in place could have on families, Matthew established a business designed to help financial advisers offer an Estate Planning service to their clients and now works with over 200 businesses throughout the UK and Northern Ireland.